BUBBA SPEAK

TEXAS FOLK SAYINGS

W. C. JAMESON

Republic of Texas Press
Plano, Texas

Library of Congress Cataloging-in-Publication Data

Jameson, W. C., 1942-
    Bubba speak : Texas folk sayings / by W. C. Jameson.
        p.   cm.
    ISBN 1-55622-616-0 (pbk.)
    1. English language—Dialects—Texas—Glossaries, vocabularies
    etc.   2. English language—Texas—Terms and phrases.
    3. Americanisms—Texas—Dictionaries.   4. Figures of speech
    —Dictionaries.   I. Title.
    PE3101.T4J35   1998   98-14817
    427'.9764—dc21   CIP

Printed in the United States of America

ISBN 1-55622-616-0
10 9 8 7 6 5 4 3 2 1
9805

All inquiries for volume purchases of this book should be addressed to
Wordware Publishing, Inc., at 2320 Los Rios Boulevard, Plano, Texas
75074. Telephone inquiries may be made by calling:

(972) 423-0090

INTRODUCTION

I vividly recall a time when I was eleven years old and sitting in a small West Texas cafe one autumn evening. I was having a late dinner on the road with my mother and watching a rare West Texas rain trying to settle the dust outside the cafe window. Mom was reading a magazine, and the dust was winning the contest with the rain. Searching for some diversion, I turned slightly to listen in on a conversation between two old men sitting at a nearby table.

The talk between the two old-timers was punctuated with an occasional wave of an arm, a tilt of a head, or a smile. Both men possessed faces deeply wrinkled by the dry desert air and the sometimes merciless sun. They each possessed a weathered look about them that somehow has always defined West Texas for me.

The two men, both in their sixties and both with a few days' growth of whiskers, owned and lived on nearby ranches. On this evening, they were discussing things related to their profession, things like windmills and cattle, barbed wire and feed. They also spoke of families and friends.

During the conversation, one of the men responded to a comment from the other by saying, "Well, I'll be a suck-egg mule!"

Introduction

At first I was startled by this unfamiliar, yet rather fascinating, expression. I leaned a bit closer and listened more intently.

With my dinner finished and my mother engrossed in her magazine, I devoted all my attention to the conversation between the two ranchers. In a short time, I was captivated, as well as amused, with their vocabularial dexterity and the ease with which they tossed out humorous, yet somehow descriptive and quite appropriate expressions. I sat enthralled, shamelessly eavesdropping on their repartee.

During the continuing exchange between the two old men, I heard one of them, referring to a son-in-law, state "when my daughter calls him he moves faster than a rooster with socks on!" A little while later, the other said his new housekeeper was "so ugly she could cook naked at deer camp and nobody would notice."

I was so tickled by these expressions and others that I wrote them down on a piece of paper as soon as I returned home that night. I placed the paper in a desk drawer, and, as the weeks went by, I added new sayings and phrases that I encountered from time to time until, after three or four years, I had accumulated about twelve pages full of them.

Occasionally, I would pull the sheets of paper out of the drawer and read over the collection, each time grinning at the sayings, sometimes laughing out loud at some of the more humorous ones. By day, I tried hard to use them in conversations.

All through my teenage years I continued to jot down new expressions as I heard them, adding significantly to the growing list. When I got to college, however, I quickly learned that such Texanisms, as I was calling my collection of sayings, were generally not appropriate to the real and *faux* intellectual discussions that flowed inside and outside of college classes. Thus, weeks, even months, passed by without any noticeable additions to the list.

While a college student, I was spending more time with intellectuals than with the salt-of-the-earth types I had grown up with. In the process, I discovered that, by and large, intellectual conversation was not nearly as colorful, descriptive, fun, or even particularly informational, as that of country folk.

During those years I was inflicting myself with higher education, I began spending a large percentage of the day exploring around the collections in libraries. Here, among the books and journals, I discovered uncountable adventures, masterpieces of writing, accounts of explorations, biographies, and cultural treatises, and likely learned more useful information than in most classes I took. I also learned, as a result of encountering several books on folklore and folkways, that the Texanisms I was collecting were called "folk sayings" by the scholars who studied them. Folk sayings, they wrote, were handed down via the oral tradition, and are expressions that are considered quite acceptable, even useful, to the folk who use them. In fact, according to the books, scholars sometimes traveled throughout the country collecting such folk sayings. The books provided examples of folk sayings from different geographic regions such as the Appalachians, the Ozarks, and the New England States.

Thus, I learned that what I was doing for pure enjoyment and simply out of curiosity turned out to a legitimate scholarly pursuit for some!

I quickly became interested in collecting more.

Texas is a wonderful place to collect almost anything as it relates to folkways and folklore. Texas covers a vast area—it consists of 267,338 square miles, about seven percent of the total land and water area of the United States. Texas contains 254 counties, some of them larger than several eastern states. The state of Texas itself is as large as all of New England, New York, Pennsylvania, Ohio, and Illinois put together.

In Texas, one can find an impressive variety of landscapes including coastal, desert, mountain, prairie grassland, and forest. Living in these environments, as of 1995, are about 18,000,000 people.

The very word "Texas" is often a metaphor, even an adjective, for something large or great or impressive. Texas is, in fact, all of these.

Texas is also filled with people, and descendants of people, who have come from an impressive variety of racial, ethnic, and cultural backgrounds. Making up much of the population of modern day Texas are Northern and Southern Anglos, Blacks, Czechs, Germans, Swiss, Italians, Russians, Mexicans, Orientals, and many, many others. A cultural mix as diverse as this is not likely to be found anyplace else in America, perhaps not even in the world.

At various periods in my life, I traveled, and continue to travel, throughout all of Texas. I travel for a number of reasons—adventure; vacation; to visit family and friends; to observe different cultures; to experience extraordinary places such as Big Bend, the Guadalupe Mountains, the Big Thicket, and the Gulf Coast. Over the years and all along the way, I collected more and more folk sayings.

When I heard new ones I wrote them down on anything available: in notebooks, on paper napkins and placemats, on the backs of receipts, in the margins of newspaper pages, and even on the back of my hand or arm when paper was not available. For the most part, the expressions contained in this book are presented exactly as they were written when I first heard them.

Over the years, patterns among these many and varied expressions became apparent. In Texas, there are lots of different ways to express ugly, useless, and unacceptable; big, boasting, bravery, and busy; happy and hot; mad and mean; poor and pretty. Interestingly, and perhaps appropriately, there are not many expressions for alone, cautious, cowardly, humble, and shy. There were no folk expressions at all for quit.

Another pattern that cropped up had to do with regional differences. Texas folk sayings from the eastern part of the state had quite a bit in common with those found in the Deep South. This should come as no surprise to cultural geographers and Southern historians since much of East Texas was settled by immigrants from Alabama, Georgia, Mississippi, Louisiana, South Carolina, and Arkansas.

Along the southern border of the Lone Star State, many sayings and phrases were found that have their counterparts in Mexico.

Likewise, sayings from North Texas and the Panhandle had a great deal in common with expressions encountered in some of the Great Plains states such as Kansas, Nebraska, and the Dakotas, as well as from the Rocky Mountain States of Colorado, Wyoming, and Montana. This is a result, the scholars tell us, of the trail drives of the mid-nineteenth century in which vast herds of Texas longhorns were driven to the railheads in the north. The cowboys who were in charge of herding the cattle brought with them into the plains and mountains their unique mode of dress, their livestock-handling techniques, and, of course, their way of expressing things—all of which became extremely popular with the residents they encountered.

Texas folk sayings are expressive, unique, extremely useful, generally colorful, oftentimes bizarre, quite descriptive, unusual, delightful, and always entertaining.

In recent years, Texanisms have been closely associated with the speech and vocabulary patterns of rural folk. Such colorful ways of expressing things have gained a great deal of attention lately and have been linked with a "redneck" segment of society, a kind of country culture, an element of the population often referred to as "Bubbas." The word "Bubba" has sometimes been employed as a derogatory or perjorative appellation, but more often than not it is used fondly. After all, the word "Bubba," is a modification of the word "Brother."

Thus, Texanisms are a form of Bubbaisms, or, perhaps more appropriately, Bubba speak!

The following manifestations of Bubba speak are an important part of the language spoken by Texans, historically and contemporarily. These terms had their origins among the fundamental root stock of early settlers to this land, those hardy, hard-working souls whose ancestors carved out a living in this sometimes harsh and forbidding environment. This is the talk of the people who have endured and survived and who will always be with us. This is the language of those who worked endlessly, sometimes excruciatingly, yet who possessed a keen and finely honed sense of humor that enabled them, in large part, to conquer the obstacles so common to those who come first.

They are kindred, in truth and in spirit. They are, in fact, our brothers.

Join me now in an excursion through the language and vocabulary of Bubba speak. Read these out loud— they sound better that way. Read them often, become familiar with them, and at every opportunity try to use them in a conversation.

A

ABANDONED

Left like last year's newspapers

As unneeded as a two-year-old bird's nest

Left out in the cold

Left out in the pasture

His family left him to be raised by wolves

Left him high and dry like a used-up oil well

ACCEPTABLE

Better than a poke in the eye with a sharp stick

Close enough for government work

Can't beat it with a stick

Took to it like a fish to water

Cookin' on the front burner

It beats pickin' cotton

It'll do till something better comes along

That dog will hunt

It beats diggin' postholes

Suits me to a fare-thee-well

That beats a hen a-scratchin'

It sure beats a hen a-lopin'

ACCIDENT-PRONE

He could fall down walkin' from the house to the barn

She once fell out of a church pew

He could cut himself with a picture of a razor

She'd fall off the rocking chair

She would run into the ladder after you
put it up in the shed

ACCURATE

Hit the nail on the head

Right as rain

Right on target

Right on the money

On the mark

Couldn't have said it better myself

Bingo

Bull's eye

ACTIVE

As a spider on a hot stove

As a chinch on a griddle

As a tick in a tar pot

As the tip of a cat's tail

As a lizard on a hot rock

As hot grease on a skillet

As a month-old puppy with no quit

Bouncin' like she's got briers in her tail

Movin' like he's got springs in his butt

Like two bobcats in a croaker sack

She moves like she was fightin' fires in her pants

Like a coon's tail when its neck's broke

As a fox in a henhouse

As a worm on a hot sidewalk

As a stump-tailed bull at fly time

He's so lively you'd think he was twins

ADVICE

It takes gizzard and guts to get along in this world

Still waters run deep and the devil lays at the bottom

If you get burnt you got to sit on the blister

Two wrongs never make a right

All the world is a goose, and them that don't
pick won't get no feathers

It don't take no big bone to choke a cow

It ain't the dog in the fight, it's the fight in the dog

Don't chew your tobacco but once

When you're up to your neck in cow manure,
don't open your mouth

When your hand is in the dog's mouth
never yank his tail

Keep your wagon between the ditches

AFRAID

Scared as a jackrabbit runnin' from a coyote

Scared as a jackrabbit in a coyote's back pocket

He took off like a jackrabbit in tall grass

He jumped like he'd stepped on a raw egg

He jumped like he just stepped on a frog

So scared his skin jumped up and crawled all over him

He'd get cold feet in the desert in the summertime

He was so scared his heart was beatin' like a
drummer with the hiccups

So afraid he swallowed his chewin' tobacco

Afraid of his own shadow

Afraid of his own face in the mirror

AGGRESSIVE

Aggressive as a fundamentalist preacher

As a snake oil salesman

As a Bible salesman

As a television preacher

As a used car salesman

As a hungry coon

As a newborn calf searchin' for his mama's teat

AGE

Older than dirt

Older than granite

Older than the Flood

Older than Methuselah

His measurin' stick is right long

He's already waded his deepest water

The spring has gone out of his chicken

He's gettin' long in the tooth

ALIKE

Squeezed from the same udder

Drained from the same crankcase

Two peas in a pod

Mixed in the same bowl

Cut from the same cloth

Not a dime's worth of difference between them

Two sheep from the same flock

Like puppies from the same litter

ALONE

As alone as a Catholic at a Baptist convention

As a ham sandwich at a Jewish picnic

As a cup of coffee at a Mormon picnic

In bad company

He rattles around like one pea in a pod

ALTERNATIVES

There's more ways to kill a hog than chokin'
him on hot butter

More than one way to skin a cat

More than one way to eat corn on the cob

More than one way to break a horse

Every coin has two sides

AMAZING

That'll blow your hat in the creek

That'll shuck your corn

That'll melt your butter

That'll snap your girdle

That'll knock you plumb off the fence

ANXIOUS

Wound up tighter than a two-dollar watch

As a little boy on Christmas Eve

As a dry steer smellin' water

APPEARANCES

She looks like an unmade bed

He looks like he was rode hard and put up wet

He looked like he had been whipped with a fence post

ARGUMENTATIVE

He'd argue with a pump handle

She'd argue with a wooden Indian

Could start a fight in an empty henhouse

He's got his tail lit up

So contrary he floats upstream

He'd argue with a fence post

ATTACK

Jump on him like ugly on an ape

Shoot with both barrels

Climb his hump with spurs on

He came on with his arms a-flailin' like windmill blades

AVOID

Dance around the problem

Avoid him like plague on a stick

If he takes the right fork, you take the left

I'd rather turn down a dirt road than
meet him on the highway

I'd travel clear to Lubbock just to avoid
meetin' him on the road

I've ducked him so much I feel like quackin'

AWAKE

As a hoot-owl

As awake as the sun

Bright-eyed and bushy-tailed

AWKWARD

She moves like a cow on crutches

As clumsy as a blind bear in a brier patch

As awkward as an elephant tryin' to use a typewriter

Like a duck out of water

As taking the in-laws on the honeymoon

She'd fall down just a-thinkin' about walkin'

B

BAD

He was soured on the cob

Rotten before he was ripe

Spoilt before he was prime

Came from a litter of barn skunks

Could drive a preacher to cuss

Lower than a snake's belly

Bad enough to be locked up *under* the jail

He's got a room reserved in hell

Mean enough to suck eggs and hide the shells

Runs with wolves and rattlesnakes

When he was born the doctor slapped him
Then he slapped the doctor back

BEATEN

Had your plow cleaned

Been sandpapered

Whipped like a red-headed stepchild

Knocked into next month

Had his tail-feathers trimmed

Beaten like a stubborn mule

Knocked cold enough to skate on

Beat bumpy

Somebody did a tap dance on his head

A big fellow did a two-step on his body

BEWARE

Katy bar the door

BIG

Big as a skinned horse

So big he looks like he ate his brother

Big as a cocklebur under the tongue

So big she has to sit down in shifts

He's big for a man but not too big for a horse

Big as Brewster County

As West Texas

As Dallas

As all outdoors

Big as a barn

Big enough to hunt bears with a switch

Big as a #4 washtub

She fills up a room like she was wearin' it

You could split him in half and still
have enough for two people

Big as a boar hog

As a wagonload

A barrel full

Big enough to hold all the sinners in church

Big enough to fill two chairs

BLIND

Blind as a bat

As a cloud

As a mole

As a day-old kitten

As a gopher

As a cactus

As a rock

As a back door

BOASTING

She can strut sitting down

All hat and no hogs

All a-gurgle and no guts

I'm a curly-tailed wolf with a pink ass

I'm a ring-tailed panther

Wild and woolly and hard to curry

He killed three preachers before he was seven years old

All wool, warp, and a yard wide

I can pry up creation and put a chunk under it

He had calluses from pattin' himself on his own back

Throwin' a lot of dust

As full of wind as a bull in corn time

Blowin' harder than a hurricane

If braggin' was food, he'd weigh 400 pounds

BOOTLEGGING

He raises more corn than ever goes to mill

Sellin' pumpkins

Haulin' the corn crop in jugs

A back road delivery man

BOOTLEG WHISKEY

Pure quill

Crow liquor

So pure you can smell the feet of the
boys that plowed the corn

Mountain dew

Rotgut

BORING

Life do get daily

Boring as a wooden Indian

Boring as a fishing trip with a game warden

Like scraping dead flies off flypaper

Bored silly

Bored witless

Conversation with her is like taking three sleepin' pills

BOWLEGGED

So bowed he couldn't stop a pig in a ditch

She looks like she's been a-carryin'
pumpkins between her knees

Banjo-legged

Bowlegged as a barrel stave

Her legs could bracket a nail keg
without touchin' the sides

BRAVERY

As brave as the first man who ate an oyster

He's got two backbones

He'd walk a tightrope without a net

He's got more guts than you could hang on a fence

Charge hell with a bucket of water

Spit in a wildcat's eye

He's got more sand than the desert

He'd fight a rattlesnake and spot it the first bite

Walk into hell alone and unarmed

Brave enough to be a first grade teacher

Brave enough to face a Mexican bull

Play tennis in a minefield

He'd wade into a bar fight with a smile on his face

BROKE

Flatter than a fritter

Couldn't buy dust

Down to my last chip

So broke he couldn't change his mind

The bank won't even let me draw breath

If money was leather, I couldn't make shoes for a mayfly

I got spiderwebs in my wallet where
my money ought to be

He ain't heard the eagle scream in over a month

BUSY

Busy as ants at a picnic

As a bee in a tar bucket

As a fly in a molasses jar

As a man with one hoe and two rattlesnakes

No grass grows under his feet

Busy as a one-legged man at an ass-kicking contest

As a one-armed paperhanger

As two coons fightin' in a tow sack

As a hen with one chicken

As a fiddler's elbow

As a hound in flea season

Busier than a one-eyed cat watchin' three mice

Busy as a buzz saw in a pine knot

As a chicken eating out of a pie pan

As a barefoot boy in an ant bed

As a bartender on payday

As a bee in a bottle

As a long-nosed weevil in a cotton patch

As a preacher countin' tithe money

C

CAPABLE

Has horse sense

She's got some snap in her garters

He could find a whisper in a whirlwind

No slack in his rope

It ain't his first rodeo

He could track a bumblebee blindfolded in a blizzard

He can pick a good horse anytime

He's got a lot of arrows in his quiver

He can find his way around Fort Worth

He's got "can do" branded on both arms

CAREFUL

Plays his cards close to the vest

Never rides more than one wagon at a time

As careful as a welder in a gasoline refinery

As a cat in a roomful of rockin' chairs

CAUTIOUS

Keeps his ear to the ground

Keeps his powder dry

Wary as a cat in a dog kennel

CELEBRATION

Shooting out the lights

Throw your hat over the chicken house

Paint the town

Paint the front porch

Be there with bells on

Hallelujah the country

Kickin' up your heels

Puttin' on the blanket

CERTAINTY

Sure as shootin'

Sure as I'm standin' here

Sure as a goose goes barefooted

Sure as a wagon wheel's round

Sure as you're born

Sure as a dead man stinks

Sure as snakes crawl

Sure as God made little green apples

That takes the whole biscuit

Lead pipe cinch

He was so certain he promised
to eat his hat, feather and all

Certain as a gut cinch

Sure as a bear has hair

As a snake slithers

Damn straight

CHARMING

She could make the old feel young
and the poor feel rich

He could charm a bird out of a tree,

the skin off a rattlesnake,

a preacher's wife out of her corset,

the legs off a table

CHEATED

He got the short end of the stick

He paid for a bull and got a billy goat

Hornswoggled

Suckered

CLEAN

Clean as a hound dog's tooth,

as a June rabbit,

as a whistle,

as a new penny,

as a boiled white shirt,

as a brand new store-bought mirror,

as a fresh-scrubbed youngster at church

CLEAR SKIES

Fairing off

Fairing up

Moderatin'

Breakin' up

CLOSE

A stone's throw away

Hollerin' distance

Close enough to share a buttonhole

Spittin' distance

CLUMSY

He couldn't hit the ground if he fell

Clumsy as a bull in a china shop,

as a three-legged cow in labor,

as a hog on ice,

as a drunk climbin' out of a bathtub

COLD

Cold as an outhouse in the winter,

as a well-digger's butt,

as a well-digger's toe,

as a well-digger's knee,

as a banker's heart

So cold the wolves are eatin' the sheep for the wool

Cold as a frog in winter,

as a witch's tit,

as a witch's kneecaps,

as a hammer in the snow

Cold as an ex-wife's heart

Cold as an ex-wife's lawyer

Cold as a mother-in-law's kiss

Cold enough to be hog killin' weather

Cold as a cast-iron commode

Cold as a pump handle in the winter

Cold as kraut

Cold as a wagon tire

Cold as a hammer

Cold as a snake

Cold as Colorado spring water

Colder than a Montana well driller

It was so cold the cows gave icicles when milked

Colder than a knot on the North Pole

Cold enough to freeze the horns off a billy goat

Cold as a snake in the deep freezer

Cold as a pawnbroker's smile

Cold enough to freeze the tail off a brass monkey

Cold enough to make cows give ice cream

Cold as a turnip

COLORS

Black as night

Black as coal

Black as the pits of hell

Black as pitch

Blacker than the heart of a pirate

Blacker than a kettle in hell

Blue as a possum's cod

Green as grass

Green as a gourd

Pea green

So green you could scrape it off

Green as sap

Green as poison

Green as a new limb

Pink as a baby's spanked butt

Red as a turkey's snout in the spring

White as the inside of a toadstool

COMMON

Common as cornbread

Common as pig tracks

Common as coon tracks on a riverbank

Common as dishwater

Common as flies on a carcass

Common as weeds in an Arkansas corn patch

COMPETENT

She could show the devil how to manage hell

He could run hell for a campground

He can read and write, figger and fight,
whup and throw down

He could put out hell with a bucket of water

He could find a whisper in a whirlwind

Could track a hornet in a hurricane

COMPLETE

That puts the lid on the jar

That makes it sundown for me

That's the whole shootin' match

Eight bits makes a buck

That brings the curtain down

That shuts the door on that deal

COMPLIMENT

You're nicer than you are ugly

You look fittin'

You look like the pick of the litter

You look a lot more like you do now
than you did when you was a while ago

CONCEITED

He's so conceited that God's overcoat
wouldn't make him a vest

He's puffed up with air

She's got flies up her nose

He thinks the sun comes up just to hear him crow

So stuck up she'd drown if it rained on her

CONFUSED

Cattywumpus in my mind

Confused as a goat on a shag carpet

I got my tongue caught in my eyeteeth and I couldn't
see what I was saying

He doesn't know a bit from his butt

Buffaloed

Barking up the wrong tree

He's driving the wrong herd to market

Confused as a woodpecker in a petrified forest

Confused as a goose huntin' thunder

Confused as a June bug on a hot griddle

Confused as a calf starin' at a new gate

Confused as a turkey with a train ticket

CONTRARY

He throws a different loop

If the sun is shinin', he'll say it's rainin'

He's a maverick

He wears straw hats in the winter and
felt hats in the summer

He marches to a different drummer

If you tossed him in the river, he'd float upstream

If you say it's sunny, she'll say it's dark

If you say gee, she says haw

CORN ON THE COB

Roastin' ears

Sweet corn

Fresh corn

Garden corn

COURTING

He's trying to tie her to the snortin' post

He's a-suffering from Cupid's cramps

She gets called on as regular as a goose goes barefooted

He's fixin' to get lady-broke

COWARDLY

Even if you melted him down,
you couldn't pour him into a fight

A cat looks big until the dog shows up

He's as yellow as mustard

He's got a yellow stripe down his back wide as his butt

CRAZY

He's got cobwebs in his attic

Crazy as a bull in a peach orchard

Crazy as a bullbat

If you put her brain in a sparrow it would fly backwards

Born on Crazy Creek

One brick shy of a load

Two pickles short of a picnic

A few pickles short of a barrel

Overdrawn at the memory bank

The porch light's on but no one's home

Crazy as a bessy bug

Missing a few buttons off his shirt

She's got a hole in her screen door

He must have been knocked in
the head with a churn dasher

Someone stole his rudder

He was full-grown in body only

Crazy as a parrot eatin' stick candy

North of his ears he was all snowdrift

Crazy as a sheepherder

He'd have to study to be a half-wit

His banjo ain't tuned right

Crazier than a pet coon

Crazier than my ex-wife

CROWDED

The place was so crowded you had
to grease your hips to turn around

So thick with people you couldn't cock a pistol

Ain't enough room to cuss a cat
without gettin' hair in your mouth

So crowded it looked like all of hell and half of Georgia

You couldn't swing a cat without hittin' something

The place was as crowded as a Baptist revival

Packed to the rafters

Packed like cows in a haulin' trailer

Crowded as sardines in a can

Crowded as hogs at the trough

So crowded you couldn't stir 'em with a stick

So crowded you had to go outside to change your mind

More crowded than an East Texas tent revival

Like havin' eight people in a telephone booth

As crowded as havin' all the in-laws for supper

D

DANCE

He dances fit to bust a gizzard string

Cuts a rug

Them gals can make their dress-tails pop

He slings a nasty ankle

Hoedownin'

Huggin' to the music

Boot scootin'

Rubbin' belt buckles

Hoofin' to the music

Smokin' them boots

Two-steppin'

Bone-shufflin'

DANGEROUS

Got a bad cat on the line

Dangerous as wearin' a metal hat in a lightnin' storm

Dangerous as peein' on an electric fence

Dangerous as wadin' in quicksand

Dangerous as walkin' barefoot on an anthill

Dangerous as ridin' a tornado bareback

Dangerous as grabbin' the wrong
end of the brandin' iron

Dangerous as milkin' a longhorn cow

Dangerous as a bobcat in your bedroll

Dangerous as tryin' to shoe a wild bronco

DARK

Dark as the inside of a coffin

Dark as a pile of black cats

Dark as a wolf's stomach

Dark as a wolf's mouth

Dark as a pocket

Dark as a sleeping bear's dream

Dark as coffee

Dark as a wad of black cats on a moonless night

So dark you couldn't find your nose with both hands

Dark as the backside of Hades

Dark as an East Texas woods on a cloudy midnight

DEATH

He's gone to buzzard bait

He traded in his banjo for a harp

Dead as Pompeii

He made peace with the ground

They pulled the green quilt over her

Deader'n a doornail

Deader'n a hammer

Deader than a crowbar

Deader'n a horseshoe

He shook hands with eternity

He's pushin' up daisies

He's answered his last roll call

He turned toes and belly up

Deader'n a lightin' bug in a milk pitcher

Deader'n hell in a preacher's backyard

Too dead to skin

Stiff as a pool cue

DEAF

Deaf as a river mussel

Deaf as an oyster

Deaf as a fence post

Deaf as thirty-year-old mule

Deaf as granite rock

Deaf as a brick

So deaf he couldn't hear thunder

So deaf he couldn't hear a train if
he was lyin' on the track

DEEP

Deeper than the world

Deeper than Jacob's well

All the way to bedrock and beyond

That hole was so deep you could hear
Chinese talkin' at the other end

Deeper than a Hill Country sinkhole

Deeper than a West Texas oil well

DEPENDABLE

He'll go to the well with you

He'll do to ride the river with

He can hold it steady in the road

Plows a straight row to the end of the field and back

DEPRESSED

He's down so low you couldn't get a jack under him

As depressing as homecoming in an orphanage

He's so low he could walk under a
trundle bed with a top hat on

Her heart was as heavy as a bucket of hog livers

My heart is as heavy as a bucket of horseshoes

He's lower than a mole's belly

So low he could jump off a nickel

He's so low he could walk under a gate

DIFFICULTY

As difficult as trying to bag flies

About as hard as puttin' butter up a
wildcat's ass with a hot awl

It's a long shot with a limb in the way

Difficult as pushin' a wet noodle through a keyhole

Hard as shinnyin' up an oak tree with an armload of eels

Hard as climbin' a greased pole with two baskets of eggs

As difficult as puttin' pantyhose on a bobcat

Hard as putting socks on a rooster

Up a creek without a paddle

It's like wadin' backwards in a high creek

It's like tryin' to teach a mermaid to do splits

Hard as sneakin' dawn past a rooster

Hard as holdin' a handful of bullfrogs

Difficult as tryin' to ride a cyclone

Difficult as tryin' to shovel out the sunshine

Difficult as plowing a wet field with a drunk mule

Difficult as pickin' fly shit out of black pepper

Difficult as playin' poker blindfolded

Difficult as tryin' to curry a bobcat with a toothache

Difficult as tryin' to lick honey off a blackberry vine

Difficult as tryin' to catch a greased pig

DISCOURAGED

As discouraged as a rice planter up a salt river

His tail is draggin' the ground

His face is long enough to eat oats out of a butter churn

DISHONEST

There are a bunch of nooses in his family tree

He's so crooked that you can't tell from
his tracks if he's coming or going

He's so dishonest he'd play cards with a politician

He'd lie on credit if he knew he
could cash it in for the truth

He can steal your money slicker
than a roomful of lawyers

He's on a first-name basis with the bottom of the deck

He don't pass all he chaws

Crooked as a dog's hind leg

Crooked as the devil's backbone

Crooked as Turkey Creek

Crooked as a pretzel

Crooked as a barrel of fish hooks

He's got faces all around his head

Couldn't trust him any farther than you could throw him

His mouth ain't no prayer book

Slippery as a pocket full of pudding

He's so crooked he has to unscrew his
socks before going to bed

He's so crooked they'll have to screw him
into his coffin when he passes away

He'd steal flies from a blind spider

DISHEVELED

He looked like he'd been drug through
a brush heap backwards

Rode hard and put up wet

Looked like a poor boy at a frolic

Rumpled

Looks like he'd been drug through the
pasture with his clothes on

DISLIKE

She hates me like a hog hates cholera

She thinks I'm lower than a cockroach's belly

She hates me worse than the devil hates holy water

She wouldn't pour water on me if I was on fire

I like her about as well as I like my mother-in-law

DISTANCE

A far piece

A fer piece

A long piece

A good piece

A middlin' piece

Up the trail a piece

Beyond yonder

Farther than you can see with the naked eye

Long as a country mile

A hoot and a holler away

A nine-iron shot away

DRINKING

I use it to rinse my mouth but I don't spit it out

Bendin' an elbow

Paintin' my tonsils with tarantula juice

He drinks enough to float a bass boat

He drinks enough to flood a badger den

He only drinks on the days that end in "y"

DRUNK

Drunker than a fiddler's bitch

When he was born he was squeezed
out of a bartender's rag

Drunker than a boiled owl

Drunker than two judges

Lit up like a church house

Snot-slinging drunk

Drunker than who-shot-John

Commode-hugging, knee-walking drunk

Drunker than Cooter Brown

Drunker than a Baptist preacher out of town

He was so drunk the world looked little to him

Drunk as a skunk

Too much mash

Skull cramps

So drunk he couldn't find his own mouth
without a leadin' string

He was so drunk he had to hold onto the grass before
he could lean against the ground

So drunk he couldn't tell wet from windy

Higher than a Georgia pine

Higher than a hawk's nest

Higher than a kite

Drunker'n a fired cowboy

Hymn-singin' drunk

Three sheets and two pillowcases to the wind

DRY

So dry the Baptists are sprinkling,
the Methodists are spitting,
and the Catholics are giving rain checks

Dry as a fish hawk's nest

Drier than the middle of a haystack

So dry the catfish are carrying canteens

Dry as a powder horn

So dry the trees are bribing dogs

Dry as an old maid's kiss

It's so dry, you'd have to prime yourself to spit

Dry as a frog under a cabbage leaf

So dry the catfish have ticks

So dry the ducks never learned how to swim

It's so dry we only got two inches
of rain during Noah's Flood

Dry as a bone

Dry as dust

Dry as El Paso County

DULL

As watching paint dry

Duller than a widow-woman's ax

Dull as chopping wood

Dull as a frow

Dull as an old hoe

As exciting as a mashed potato sandwich

Dull as a week-old beer

No speed, no sparkle

If'n he was bacon, he wouldn't sizzle
if you left him on the fire all day

His knife is so dull you could ride
to the mill on it with no blanket

DUMB

So dumb he spits upwind

If brains were leather he wouldn't have
enough to saddle a flea

Dumb as a sack of stones

Dumb as a bucket of rocks

Dumb as dirt

Dumb as dirt on a stick

There's a big gap in his hedge

If brains were bacon, he wouldn't even sizzle

If brains were ink, she couldn't dot an i

If brains were dynamite, he couldn't blow his nose

If you put his brain in a bumblebee,
it would fly backwards

He's so ignorant that when he tells you
howdy he's told you all he knows

Dumb as a post

Tryin' to teach him somthin' is like
poundin' sand in a rathole

Tryin' to teach her somethin' is like
chasin' a chigger around a stump

He carries his brains in his coat pocket

Dumb as a watermelon

He don't know big wood from kindlin'

So dumb she can't tell "come here" from "sic 'em"

So dumb he could screw up an anvil

He was out behind the barn when they
passed out the brains

So dumb he couldn't teach a hen to cluck

He has as many brains as a turtle has feathers

He couldn't drive a nail in a snowbank

He's got the brains of grasshopper

She's got the brains of a gnat

He couldn't track an elephant in ten feet of snow

There ain't nothin' under his hat but hair

He ain't the sharpest knife in the drawer

He's dumb enough to be twins

He'd have to study a week just to be stupid

He has the IQ of a gourd

He has the IQ of a Brazos River mussel

He's as smart as a catfish: all mouth and no brains

She couldn't count to twenty with her socks off

She ain't got a lick of sense

He don't know gee from haw

E

EAGER

He jumped on that like a duck on a June bug

He's hot to trot and already a-saddled

EASY

No hill for a climber

Easy as peach pie

Dead easy

Easy as fallin' off a log

Easy as sellin' watermelons in July

Easy as a cat climbin' a tree

Piece of cake

Easy as shooting ducks in a barrel

Easy as catchin' fish in a barrel

Easy as catchin' fish with dynamite

EMPTY

Empty as a dead man's eyes

Empty as a preacher's head

Empty as a chicken farmer's bank account

Empty as a banker's heart

Empty as a brassiere hangin' on the clothesline

Empty as last year's bird nest

Empty as an old maid's dreams

Empty as a cotton sack in January

EXAGGERATE

Pourin' short sweetenin' into long

Gildin' the rose

She was known to stretch the blanket

His facts are made out of elastic

He can puff up the truth so you hardly recognize it

EXCITED

Her bobbin is wound tight

He's stoked up like a steam engine

Runnin' around like a chicken with its head cut off

Jumpin' around like a lizard on a hot griddle

She was so excited the wax popped out of her ears

Settin' the woods on fire

Excited as a calf in new clover

Excited as a bug in a tater patch

EXCLAMATION

Well, slap the dog and spit in the fire!

Cut my legs off and call me shorty!

Well don't that take the whole biscuit!

Well, I'll be a blue-nosed gopher!

I'll be hornswoggled!

I'll be jiggered!

I'll be dipped!

F

FAILURE

Blames everybody but himself

His well rope keeps breakin'

She can't make the grade

He keeps gettin' caught in his own loop

He never makes it to the fast lane,
he's always drivin' on the shoulder

He couldn't pass muster with a ten-day head start

FAITHFUL

He's been wed to the same notions all his life

He'll dance with who he brung

You can count on her like warts on a frog

He's as faithful as an old hound dog

FAMILIAR

I've already been through that weed patch

I believe I've howdied and shook with him before

I believe me and him watered
at the same trough before

I'd recognize his ashes in a hurricane

I'd know him if he went to town
and came back dandied

I've been down that road before

We were as close as if we had been raised
on the same side of the mountain

Shook from the same tree

FAR

So far away you'd need to pack a lunch

They live forty-five miles from Austin by telephone

They live so far away you'd have to ride a pregnant
mule to get there so you could have a way to return

So far away that overnight mail takes a month

He lives so far away that him and horizon are buddies

A bunch of yonders

Go to the sunset and travel another half-day

FAST

He moved like a duck on a June bug

Quick as a bunny

Quick out of the chute

Fast as a New York minute

Fast as a new Ford

Fast as small town gossip

Fast as greased lightning

Goin' like pigs after a pumpkin

If he had feathers he'd a-been flyin'

Fast enough to grab rabbits before
they can get word to God

Quicker than Christ can get the news

Faster than a prairie fire with a tail wind

Faster than a scalded cat

If he was any faster he'd catch up with yesterday

Faster than half of no time

Fast as forty goin' north

Runnin' like the mill-tails of hell

Runnin' like a striped-ass ape

Packin' the mail

Lickety split

Faster'n a rattlesnake strike

Faster'n a Texas blue norther tearin'
through the Panhandle

FAT

She ain't missed no meals

She's expectin' a hard winter

He's got a gut like a rain barrel

He looms up like a barn in the fog

Four ax-handles across the butt

She favors a barrel

She's all swole up like a poisoned pup

Swelled up like a cow on bloat weed

He was built like a tub of lard

She's so fat she has to put her panties on with a winch

Her dress is big enough for a tent full of gypsies

Pumpkin-bellied

That fella was so fat you couldn't see his eyes

She's so fat she gets in her own way

Like a cat full of kittens

Fat as a hog during butcherin' season

Fat as a boardinghouse rat

It'd take a big loop to rope her

Grained up and ready to ship

He can walk a wide path

He's heavy in the middle and poor at the ends

The tongue and buckle of his belt
ain't seen each other in years

She's got an ass as fat as a river bottom raccoon

Fat as Aunt Eppie's hog

FEEL GOOD

If I felt any better, I'd black out

If I felt any better, I'd be arrested

Feelin' top drawer and bowl full

I feel candy bar good

I feel good enough to dance the
hokey pokey all by myself

FENCES

That fence is horse high, bull strong,
pig tight, and goose proof

His fence is so crooked a drunk man must have built it

His fence was so tight you could pluck a tune on it

His fence is tighter than ol' lady Watson's girdle

FERTILE

As fertile as bottomland on the Brazos

You could plant a nail and grow a horseshoe

That land is so fertile you could
plant toothpicks and grow lumber

That land is as fertile as last year's feed lot

FIGHT

A Pecos promenade

A Zaragoza two-step

Disagreement

A barn-burner

FIGHTER

He could whip his weight in wildcats

He could lick a chainsaw

He'll kick your butt until your teeth fall out

He'll fight at the drop of a hat

He's a curly wolf

He's a roadhouse rowdy and mean enough
to bite through horseshoes

FINE

Finer'n frog hair

Finer'n frog hair split four ways and sanded

Fine as split silk

Fine as dollar cotton

Fine as the head hair on a newborn baby

FLAT

Flat as a fritter

Flat as a pancake

Flat as the Panhandle plains

Flat as Dumas

Flat as an ironing board

Flat as a deck of cards

Flat as a cat on the highway

Flat as a wallet a week after payday

FLOOD

Five feet high and rising

Hub deep to a tall wagon

Enough water to make Noah's Flood
look like a swimming pool

Enough water to move big rocks

FOOD

Chuck

Chow

Grub

Slop

Rations

Vittles

FRIEND

Pal

Amigo

Pardner

Pard

Compadre

Sidekick

Buddy

As long as I got a biscuit, he can have half

Neighbor

He's always got his welcome mat out

FRUSTRATED

Makes you want to bang your head
against a wall

In a lather

Frustrated as the seventh piglet
of a six-teated sow

Frustrated as a chicken tryin' to
drink water out of a pie pan

FULL

Full as a wood tick

Full as a bullbat

Full as a June goat

Side-lappin' full

Brim full

Three belt notches full

Filled to the eyelashes

So full he'll have to be wheelbarrowed home

FUN

Ain't had this much fun since the
hogs ate my little brother

More fun than chasin' armadillos

Knee-slappin' fun

G

GAIT

Walks like he's belly deep in ice water

Struts like she's got a corncob between her legs

Staggers like a buckeyed calf

Walks like he's comin' through briers

Walks like a chicken in deep oats

Walks like an old hen

She's got a hitch in her get-along

She runs like a chicken pullin' a wagon

He walks like his bones were made of rubber

Jigger-legged

Loose-limbed

GENEROUS

She has a heart as soft as summer butter

He'd give you the food off'n his plate

He'd give you his shirt off'n his back

He'd empty his wallet for you if you
needed what was inside

GENTLE

Gentle as a lamb

Gentle as a kitten

Gentle as a fawn

Gentle as a kid (goat)

Gentle as a carousel horse

Gentle as a newborn colt

GHOST

Spook

Haint

Speert

Booger

Goblin

GOSSIP

That woman's mouth is always movin'
like the south end of a goose

When she talks it sounds like a
bumblebee in a dry gourd

Hangin' out dirty washin'

His mouth was a-goin' like a cotton gin in pickin' time

Loose talk

Moccasin talk

Back fence talk

Tongue waggin'

Jaw flappin'

Yammerin'

GUARANTEE

Lead pipe cinch

As sure as a chicken has feathers

As certain as a bear has hair

You can bet your bottom dollar

You can bet the ranch on that

You can bet your mama and her kids

You can bet your next born child on that

GREETING

Light down and cool your saddle

How's your tobacco taste today?

Take a load off

Toss down your pack

Set and light a spell

GUILTY

Guilty as sin

Looked as guilty as an egg-suckin' hound

He got caught with his hand in the till

He got caught with his hand in the cookie jar

She got caught red-handed

H

HAIRY

Hairy as a summer ground hog

Hairy as Ned in the first reader

HANDSOME

He has to fight 'em off with a wet tow sack

Good lookin' enough to take home to mama

Knee-wobblin' good lookin'

He could be in a magazine with that face

HANDY

Handy as a pocket on a pair of pants

Handy as the zipper on your Levis

Handy as a ladder on a windmill

Handy as a Braille Bible to a blind sinner

HANGED

Noosed

Strung up

Texas collar

Cottonwood decoration

Dressed in hemp

Neck-hemped

Guest of honor at a string party

Human fruit

Rope meat

Necktie party

Tree trimmin'

Texas cakewalk

Danglin' from an oak

HAPPY

Happy as a boardinghouse pup

Happy as a heifer in a corncrib

Happy as a hog in slop

Happy as a pig in a peach orchard

Happy as a hog in a mud hole

Happy as a clam in high tide

Happy as a skunk in a churn

Happy as a possum in a pie

Happy as a turkey in young corn

Grinnin' like a mule eatin' thistles

Happy as a puppy with two tails

Happy as a cat in a creamery

Happy as a little boy on Santa's lap

Happy as a horned toad on an anthill

Happy as a kid in a candy store

Happy as a toad under a drippy faucet

Happy as a kid on Christmas morning

HARD

Hard as a horseshoe

Hard as ironwood

Hard as a frozen wheel hub

Hard as a crowbar

Hard as a bois d'arc log

Hard as granite

HARD TO DO

Hard as eatin' creamed corn with a pitchfork

Hard as pushin' a wheelbarrow with rope handles

Hard as butcherin' a hog with a dull knife

Hard as threadin' a needle in a dark cellar

HARD WORKER

He wears out two pairs of gloves a day

He works from can't see to can't see

He'll wear out a young mule

He'll give you a day's work for a day's pay

HEAVY

Heavy as an anvil

Heavy as an anchor

Heavy as a tow sack full of ball bearings

Heavy as ol' lady Bartram's oldest daughter

HIDDEN

There's a squirrel in that tree somewhere

There's a bug under that chip

Squirreled away

Stashed

HONESTY

So honest you could play poker
with him over the telephone

If he says it, you can take it to the bank

Talkin' turkey

Can hang your hat on what he says

If that ain't the truth,
you can cut me up for catfish bait

Honest as the day is long

Shootin' square

Bone-limbed

HOT

Hot as a tater

Hot as hell

Hot as a firecracker

Hot as a parsnip

Hotter than the hinges of hell

Hot as fire in a pepper mill

Hotter'n a habanero

Feels like hell ain't half a mile away
and the fences are all down

Hotter than a pistol

Hot as a run-down billy goat

Hotter than a billy goat in a pepper patch

Hot as a red hen

Hotter than hell with the lid screwed down

Hot as a hen layin' a goose egg

Hotter than a revival in July

Hot as a red beet

Hotter than a preacher's knee

Hotter than a fur coat in August

Hot as a stolen tamale

Hot as a burning stump

Hotter than a honeymoon hotel

So hot the potatoes are bakin' in the ground

So hot the corn is poppin' on the stalk

Hot as a black Cadillac in July

Hottern' road tar on a July afternoon

Hottern' a depot stove

Hottern' Hell's door handle

Hot enough to melt leather

Hot enough to melt limestone

Hot enough to melt an anvil

Hot enough to wilt a fence post

Hot enough to fry spit

HUMBLE

He was raised with ticks in his navel

He walks around with his hat in his hand

HUNGRY

That gal eats so much she stays skinny
just carryin' all that weight around

He's got the miss-meal cramps

His stomach is so empty it sounds hollow
when you thump it

I'm so hungry my backbone and belly button
shook dice to see which would have the first bite

So hungry I could eat windmill blades

Hungry enough to eat a saddle blanket

Hungry as a billy goat in a bare pasture

Hungry as a coyote in a drought

Hungry enough to eat a cast-iron skillet

Hungry enough to eat a bear with the hair still on it

I'm so hungry I could eat a frozen dog

I

IGNORANT

He don't know beans when the poke's open

He can't tell his hand in front of his face

He couldn't find his butt with both hands

He's got the IQ of a fence post

He's got the IQ of a pigeon

He don't know cream from butter

He don't know big wood from kindlin'

He's divin' in shallow water

He don't know gunpowder from pepper

He don't know hamburger from mouse turds

He doesn't have the sense God gave a goose

She doesn't have the sense God gave a monkey wrench

In a battle of wits he'd be unarmed

If you put his brain in a grasshopper, it'd hop backwards

He ain't got the brains God gave an oyster

IMMORAL

She's loose as ashes in a windstorm

Wilder than a yard full of snakes

Hitched but not churched

They planted their crops before they built their fence

They call her "radio station" because
you can pick her up at night

His morals got a leak in 'em somewhere

She'd take up with a snake if it
promised her a good time

IMPORTANT

He bores with a big auger

He's a big frog in a small pond

He's the tush hog of the herd

She's chief cook and bottle washer

He's tall dog in the pack

He's the lead bull

He's the bull goose of the flock

IMPOSSIBLE

You can't float an anvil

That's as impossible as findin'
horse thieves in heaven

That's as impossible as hatchin' a
rooster from a robin's egg

You can't make a silk purse out of a sow's ear

Might as well sing psalms over a dead horse

Might as well try to eat soup with a knife

Might as well try to eat sugar
with a knitting needle

INAPPROPRIATE

Like a poor boy at a frolic

Like a prostitute in Sunday school

Like a ham sandwich at a Jewish picnic

Like a drunk at a Pentecostal service

Like a cup of coffee at a Mormon picnic

INCOMPETENT

He's such a bad farmer he can't raise Cain

Day late and a dollar short

He can't win for losing

He can't see for lookin'

He couldn't knock a hole in the wind with a
wheelbarrow full of hammers

She'd mess up a two-car funeral

Worthless as two buggies in a one-horse town

She couldn't hit the floor if she fell out of bed

As useless as a needle without an eye

He couldn't drive a nail into a snowbank
with a sledgehammer

She'd drown in the shower if she wasn't careful

He can't spit past his chin

He don't know shine shindig

INDEPENDENT

She's as independent as a hog on ice

He rolls his own loop

He paddles his own canoe

He saddles his own horse

He strings his own fence

He fries his own bacon

He'll take his foot in hand and walk

INEXPERIENCED

He's so green, if it was springtime
the cows would eat him

He just rode in on a pulpwood truck

He fell off the back of a turnip truck

He just come in on a watermelon truck

Still wet behind the ears

He's so green he could hide in a lettuce field

Green as a gourd

Green as grass

Green as a new shoot on a young oak

INFIDELITY

That bull's in the wrong pasture

There's an odd mule in a strange stall

There's a different horse tied to the hitch rail

INSULTS

Even a blind hog can find an acorn once in a while

Were you raised by hogs?

Were you raised in a barn?

Were you raised by truckers?

Were you raised by wolves?

Were you raised by rednecks?

Were you raised by moonshiners?

What did you do with the money your mother
gave you for manners lessons?

Anytime you pass by my house I would appreciate it

He has all of the qualities of a dog except loyalty

She don't sweat much for a fat gal

INTELLIGENT

He's got more information in his head
than a Sears catalog

Smarter than a ten-year-old cat

Smart as a whip

He knows not to pee on an electric fence

He can tell a stallion from a gelding

J

JAIL

Lockup

Pokey

Hoosegow

Calaboose

Jug

Clink

Cooler

Can

Iron

Cross-bar hotel

JOIN

To hook up with

Throw your hat in the ring

Toss your hat on my nail

Sign up

Put your oar in the boat

Put your saddle in my barn

Drop your rope with mine

In bed together

Put your horse in my barn

Put your horse in my corral

Turn your horse out in my herd

JUMP

He jumped like a rangy bull
out of chute number three

He jumped as high as a dynamited tree stump

Jumpin' around like frog legs in a fryin' pan

He can jump like he's got springs in his boots

Jumps like a frog on vitamins

Jumps like a nervous jackrabbit

K

KIDDING

Pullin' my leg

Twistin' the truth

Shuckin' me with your stories

Rawhiding

Razin'

Hoorawin'

Joshin'

Bullshittin'

Funnin'

Makin' sport

KILL

Do away with

Hold under water

L

LAWYER

A hungry shark

Ambulance chaser

A piranha in a suit

A buzzard in a three-piece suit

Pick pocket

Legal worm

LAZY

He hangs out more than mama's wash

They call him "blister" because he shows up
when the work is done

Lazy as a shingle-maker

He was born tired and raised lazy

He's so lazy he has to stop plowin' to poot

He's so lazy he has to prop himself up to cuss

Too lazy to steal

He's not afraid of hard work, cause I've seen him lay
down and go to sleep right next to it

She's too light for heavy work
and too heavy for light work

He's too lazy to shoo the flies off himself
when he's a-sleepin' on the porch

Lazy as a pet coon

Lazy as a twenty-five-year-old blue tick hound

Lazier'n Uncle Jack's wife

He's too lazy to knock flies out of his mouth

Too lazy to shuck corn if you gave it to him

LEADER

Bell mare

Bell cow

Boss man

Big dog

Top gun

Top hand

Head eagle

The captain

Bull goose

LEAVING

Light a shuck

Make tracks

Move 'em on out

Hit the road

Vamoosing

Chasing the sunset

Set your back to the wind and let it take you

Strike out

Hightail it

Light out

Goin' to the house

Goin' to the barn

Pullin' freight

Raisin' dust

Jumpin' the traces

Church is out

Headed for the wagon yard

Time to put out the fire and call the dogs

Hit the road

It's time to put the chairs in the wagon

Goin' to the corral

LIAR

I wouldn't believe him if he swore
on a stack of Bibles a mile high

He's prone to whiff

He'd sooner climb a tree to tell a lie
as stand on the ground and tell the truth

LIQUOR

Firewater

Tarantula juice

Bug juice

Rot gut

Kickapoo joy juice

Snakebite remedy

Patent medicine

Panther piss

Tiger piss

Rumble juice

Crazy water

Mare's milk

Tiger milk

Antifreeze

Solvent

Throat coat

Tonsil melt

LONG

Long as a well rope

From here to yonder and back

From here to yesterday and back

Long as a Texas mile

Long as a wagon trail

A good piece

A good ways

From here to Kansas and back

To hell and gone

LOST

Lost as a goose

Lost as a turkey in the corn

Couldn't find his ass with both hands

Couldn't find his ass with a bloodhound

Couldn't find his ass in a telephone booth

Couldn't find his ass if he had a cord tied to it

He couldn't find his ass in a washtub

LOUD

You can't hear your ears in this place

Sounds like the Fourth of July in a bedroom

Loud enough to drown out my mother-in-law

Loud enough to cause a horned toad to go deaf

He had a voice like the bulls of Bashan

LOVE

I'd wade knee-deep in blood to get to that gal

He'd crawl on broken glass to get to that gal

I've taken to her like a lean tick to a fat dog

She took to him like a sick kitten to a hearthstone

He's so in love he'd wash her feet and drink the water

He's got some heart-bustin' feelin's

LUCKY

When he sits on the fence the birds feed him

He could draw a full house from a stacked deck

If they hung him, the rope would break

Riding the gravy train with biscuit wheels

He'd strike oil while diggin' a grave

He could fall into the outhouse
and come out smellin' like a Tyler rose

He always draws an ace

He walks in the sun on cloudy days

MAD

Mad as a coon in a poke

Mad as a bullfrog on a tack

He's got his tail up

Mad as a sow with sore tits

Madder than if he found a hair in the butter

Madder than a settin' hen

On the prod

Blown up like a toad

On the warpath

Mad enough to eat fire ants

Mad enough to eat rattlesnakes

Mad enough to eat bees

Madder than a wet hen

Cross as a bear with two cubs

Riled

Mad as a bee-stung dog

Cross as a bear with a sore tail

Lathered

Mad enough to toss a bull

Mad enough to kick a mule barefooted

Mad enough to butt stumps

He's startin' to bellow and paw dust

She's all horns and rattles

Mad as a rooster in an empty hen house

Mad enough to kick his own dog

Boilin'

Mad enough to bite the head off a hammer

Mad enough to chew an anvil

Mad enough to eat nails

Mad as a preacher with the devil
camped out in his yard

She's got her dander up

Her nails are flashin' and her tail's a-twitchin'

Mad as a fightin' rooster

Her purr has turned to a growl

He's hotter than coals in a train depot stove

He's burnin' some powder

He's got his holster tied down

Walkin' mad

Mad enough to throw a walleyed fit

He's got itchy fangs

Jumpin' mad

Hoppin' mad

MANY

So many you couldn't stir 'em with a stick

Like ants on a dead snake

Like relatives at a dead oilman's funeral

As many as Texas has oil wells

As many as Texas has pretty girls

As many as Carter has little liver pills

As many as Baptists at a testimonial

MARRIED

Carryin' a brand

Hitched

Webbed

Trottin' along in a double harness

Roped

Yoked

Holy bedlock

Harnessed

Bridled and tied

MEAN

So mean he'd steal the nickels off a dead man's eyes

Bucksnortin' mean

Mean enough to spit poison

Mean enough to steal his mama's Christmas money

Ornery

He'd steal flowers off a fresh grave

Huntin' trouble with a big gun

He cut his teeth on cast-off spikes

Stirrin' up hell with a long spoon

Mean as a wasp

Mean as a snake

So mean he'd cut you up into little pieces
and send you to the undertaker collect

Mean as a bulldog on a gunpowder diet

He must've been suckled by a she-wolf
with four tits and holes punched for more

His stinger's half out

Mean enough to steal a widow's ax

Mean as a bobcat in a burlap sack

Mean as a skunk

Meaner than dockroot

Mean as gar broth

Mean enough to bite himself

Mean as a chicken-eatin' hog

Mean as a wasp with two stingers

Meaner'n a hungry pit bull

MISTAKE

Hung the wrong cattle rustler

Lassoed the wrong steer

Caught in his own beaver trap

Barked up the wrong tree

Saddled somebody else's horse

Pulled his trigger without aiming

Put his foot in the wrong boot

Tied up to the wrong hitchin' post

MUDDY

So muddy it would bog down a snipe

So muddy I sank to my knees

So muddy it would bog down a buzzard's shadow

That water's so muddy you could track a coon
down the middle of the creek

MURDER

Put a spider in his coffee

Put a spider in his biscuit

N

NAKED

Naked as a jaybird

Naked as a plucked goose

Nekkid

Buck naked

Butt naked

She ain't got nothin' on but the radio

Naked as the day is long

Naked as the day she was born

Naked as a buzzard's head

Naked as a scalded hog

I seen more of her than the law allows

NERVOUS

Nervous as a long-tailed cat in a
room full of rockin' chairs

Nervous as a pregnant mule

Nervous as a whore in church

Nervous as a pig in a packing plant

Nervous as a fly in a glue pot

Nervous enough to sweat bullets

Nervous as a grass widow at a camp meetin'

Squirmin' like a worm in hot ashes

Shakin' so much she could thread the needle on a
sewing machine while it was runnin'

Sweatin' like a bound boy at a corn-shuckin'

Shakin' like a heifer with her first calf

Shakin' like a hog eatin' charcoal

Nervous as a politician on Judgement Day

Nervous as a preacher on Judgement Day

NEVER

It'll be a cold day in Hell

In a pig's eye

When Hell freezes over

When the Rocky Mountains go flat

When the Brazos River dries up

When palm trees grow in the Panhandle

NIMBLE

Nimble as a weasel

Nimble as a young dancer

Nimble as a green snake

NOISY

Noisy as a mad mule in a metal barn

Noisy as two skeletons dancing on a tin roof

As noisy as a cornhusk mattress

Noisy as ducks on a new feed ground

Noisy as a mule eatin' charcoal

Noisy as a windmill needin' oil

Noisy as feedin' time at the hog pen

Noisy as a pig caught under a gate

Noisy as two range bulls fightin' in a cornfield

NONE OF YOUR BUSINESS

Fattenin' frogs for snakes

Makin' kitten britches for tomcats

Makin' popovers to catch meddlers

None of your beeswax

None of your cornbread

None of your she-tacks

Huntin' hoot owls

Go climb a stump

NONSENSE

Turkey hooves

Horse feathers

Bull feathers

Hogwash

A crock

Steer's milk

Hooey

Bullshit

Rigmarole

Buffalo chips

O

OBSTACLE

He hit a knot

That hill got higher

Somebody throwed a sprag in his wheel

Like a stump in a corn patch

Like saddlin' a tall horse

Like saddlin' an angry mule

Like climbin' a tall fence

Like tryin' to move a bull out of the kitchen

OBVIOUS

I could tell that's the way it was
with one hand tied behind my back

Plain as the nose on your face

Plain as the cards on the table

Plain as day

You don't have to tell a duck
what to do with corn

You don't have to tell a cat
what to do with a mouse

Plain as a dog turd on a bedsheet

If it had been a snake it would of bit you

OLD

Old-timer

Old as God

Old as rock

Old as dirt

Old as Methuselah

Old as sin

He's old enough to be a grandaddy to an oak tree

Old as black pepper

He's got lines in his face from tryin' to
straighten out the wrinkles in his life

He's old enough to have been a
waiter at the Last Supper

He's a gummer

Fogey

Geezer

Codger

OUTRAGEOUS

It's a sight for the world

That's a sketch for the birds

A long way from ordinary

OVER

It ain't over until the shoutin's done
and they gather up the singin' books

It ain't over till the preacher says it's over

It ain't over until all the horses are back in the corral

P

PANTS

Levi's

Trousers

Britches

Breeches

Jeans

Denims

PATIENCE

Take a tater and wait

Don't get your underpants in a wad

He'll lean against the rack until the fodder falls

He's as patient as a buzzard circling a sick calf

He don't count the crop till it's in the barn

PERSEVERANCE

If you mind your knittin',
you'll soon have a sweater

If he can't lead a horse to water,
he'll bring water to the horse

He's got the cleanest fence rows in the county

PERSUASIVE

He could take a bone away from a hungry dog

He could sell a car to a blind woman
who didn't live near a road

He could gentle a mustang just by talkin' to it

He could talk a green tree into kindlin'

PLAYFUL

Playful as a kitten

Playful as a colt in clover

Playful as a puppy on the porch

Playful as a pet raccoon

PLENTIFUL

Beaucoup
(pronounced boo-coo)

Heap

Passel

Gob

Wagonload

A mess of

A sackful

Potload

Bunch

More than adequate

POACHING

Jailhouse deer

Them trout was caught on a silver hook

That ain't deer, that's goat mutton

POLICE

Lawmen

Johnny Law

The Rangers

Ticket pushers

Bears

Smokeys

Badge-toter

Fuzz

Pigs

POOR

Poor as a lizard-eating cat

Poor as buzzard dung

So poor he had a pinecone for a pet

They had nothin' but skim milk and wild onions

They was so poor they was drinkin' branch water
and eatin' sheep sorrel

They live mostly on fallen apples and dry wind

They was so poor they couldn't buy a nightmare

They didn't have nothin' but their feet on the ground

We had oatmeal for breakfast, cornmeal for dinner,
and miss-a-meal for supper

We'd rattle the dishes and fool the cats

Poor as a church house mouse

Poor as a sawmill rat

So poor he had to fertilize the sill
before he could raise the window

If a trip around the world cost a dollar
I couldn't get to the Arkansas state line

Too poor to pay attention

Too poor to paint, too proud to whitewash

So poor the wolf wouldn't stop at their door

So poor he couldn't buy worms for a sick hen

They ain't got a pot to pee in

He was so poor he had to wear
a straw hat at Christmas

He was so poor he had a tumbleweed for a pet

He was so poor he couldn't make a
down payment on a fishin' worm

Poor as Job's turkey

Poor as a West Texas pineapple farmer

PREGNANT

She's got a bun in the oven

She's totin'

She's settin' a nest

Heiferized

She done made her crop

She's got one in the chute

She's been storked

She swallered a watermelon

She swallered a punkin seed

Hollerin' pappy down the rain-barrel

PRETTY

Pretty as a speckled pup

She's so pretty she could make a man plow
through a field of stumps

Pretty as a goggle-eyed perch

Pretty as a new-laid egg

Pretty as a fence-corner peach

Built like a brick outhouse

A looker

So pretty she'll blind your eyes and break your heart

She's fixed up like a jaybird at pokeberry time

Pretty as a bug's ear

She has more curves than a yard full of fishhooks

Pretty as a speckled pup in a red wagon

Pretty as a bald-faced heifer

Pretty as a pie supper

So pretty I'd rather look at her than eat breakfast

Pretty as a baby's smile

Prettier than a striped snake

Prettier than a silver dollar

Pretty as a red heifer in a flowerbed

She looks like a mail order catalog with feet

Pretty as a picture

Pretty as a field of bluebonnets

PRIDE

Proud as a peacock with two tails

His britches are ridin' high

She's struttin' like a hen at layin' time

Proud as a puppy with a new collar

She had pride so thick an axe wouldn't cut it

That ol' hen thinks her chicks are the finest

She's all swole up like a frog in the butter churn

Puffed up like a pigeon in a bow tie and tux

PROBLEM

He's got a big hole in his chicken fence

He's got locusts in his axle grease

He's got wasps in the outhouse

His ox is in the ditch

He loaded the wrong wagon

There's a mouse in the meal

We got a fly in the ointment

Somebody dropped a can o' pepper
in the butter churn

PROSPEROUS

No cobwebs in her purse

Livin' high on the hog

Livin' in tall cotton

Where the pancake tree grows
beside the honey pond

Well-fixed

She sneezes through silk

Cuttin' the big jimson

Q

QUANTITY

More than Carter had liver pills

More than Carter had oats

More than Iowa has corn

A mess

A slew

More than you can shake a stick at

More than all the sand grains in West Texas

More than all the cotton in Texas

QUICK

Quick as greased lightnin'

Quicker than double-greased lightnin'

Quick as chain lightnin'

Quicker than double-geared lightnin'

Quicker than two gods can skin a minnow

Quick as a snake goin' through a hollow log

Quicker than you can say God with your mouth open

Quicker'n a road runner on a rattlesnake

Quicker than the snap of a bullwhip

Quick as a hiccup

Quicker'n the strike of a rattler

QUIET

Quiet as a mouse

Quiet as a butterfly

Quiet as a breeze

Quiet as a whisper

Quiet as death

So quiet you could hear hair grow

So quiet you could hear grass grow

So quiet you could hear the heartbeat
of a hummingbird

Quiet as a graveyard

Quiet as a mouse pissin' on a cotton boll

Quiet as a snowflake landin' on a feather

So quiet you could hear a gnat scratch

Quiet as a sweet dream

QUITTING

Pullin' up stakes

Rollin' up the lariat

Cashin' in

Takin' off my spurs

Callin' it a day

Pullin' off the saddle

Hangin' up my hat

Rollin' my bedroll

Turnin' in my company mare

R

RAIN

Duck weather

Duck drowner

Goose drowner

Toad strangler

Dam buster

Fence-lifter

Turd floater

Rainin' cats and dogs

Rainin' bull frogs

Rainin' heifer yearlings

RARE

Rare as warm day in January

Rare as bluebonnets in January

Rare as a white crow

Rare as hen's teeth

Rare as toad hair

Rare as water in the desert

Rare as fangs on a duck

Rare as feathers on a snake

Rare as ice water in hell

Rare as snow in August in Houston

Rare as a rainy day in Huspeth County

RARE MEAT

Just sear the edges

I've seen steers cut worse than this get well

Knock the horns off and lay it on the grill for a minute

RECKLESS

Reckless as a bull in a china closet

Reckless as a puppy in a roomful of little kids

RECOGNITION

I'd know your hide in a tan yard

I'd know him in a dark room with the lights out

RELAX

Take a load off

Breathe easy

Pull your shirttail out

Rest easy

Hunker down a spell

Set a spell

RELIABLE

If he says a chicken dips snuff,
you'll find a snuffbox under its wing

He's right as rain and certain as sin

You can take that to the bank

If he says a piglet can pull a boxcar,
then you can start hitchin' 'em up

He's as reliable as a railroad watch

REMOTE

Lived so far out in the country
he had to go toward town to hunt

The place looked like a desert with
everyone out to lunch

They live out where the buses don't run

He lives out on the backside of nowhere

REPEAT

Lick that calf all over again

Ride down that path once more

Run that remuda by me one more time

Whip that dog for me once more

REST

Take some shade

Cool your heels

RESTLESS

He wanders like a bug on a hot night

Restless as a squirmin' kid at Sunday school

He's got ants in his pants

You couldn't tie him down with a stout rope

Chompin' at the bit

Restless as a chicken on a hot stove

RETIRED

Put out to pasture

Traded in his gold watch for a rockin' chair

He's got lots of time and nothin' to do with it

He done joined the spit and whittle society

RIDICULOUS

Ridiculous as pourin' water on a rusty wheel bearing

Ridiculous as trying to catch raindrops in fish net

Ridiculous as puttin' a fire out with kerosene

RILED

He got his underwear in a knot

She busted her bloomers

Put on the war paint

Went off half-cocked

She's got her horns out

RISK

I'll make a spoon or spoil a horn

He'd sit on a powder keg a-smokin' a cigarette

It'll cure or kill

He's sawin' off the limb he's settin' on

Risky as sittin' under a lightnin' rod
during a thunderstorm

Risky as dancin' with your best friend's wife

ROPE

Lariat

Maguey

Manila

String

Cow catcher

Horse catcher

ROUGH

Rougher than a cow's tongue

Rough as a corncob

Rough as cedar bark

Rough as barbed wire underwear

Rough as 'gator hide

Rough as the sole of a barefooted wetback

Rough as a washboard road

Rough as an old railroad bed

RUDE

She ain't got manners enough to carry guts to a bear

She was under the porch when they
passed out the manners

Poor mannered

RUN

Cut a chogie

Foggin'

Burnin' leather

Burnin' daylight

Beatin' it

Runs like a scalded cat

Splittin' the wind

Runs fast as a roadrunner chased by a coyote

Runs fast enough to catch yesterday

RUTHLESS

He kicks ass, takes names, and shoots the wounded

He has the conscience of an assassin

His blood is as cold as ice

He'd stake his daddy to an anthill

S

SACK

Tow sack

Gunny sack

Croaker sack

Grass sack

Feed sack

SAD

He looks like the cheese fell off'n his cracker

Eyeball waterin'

He eats sorrow by the bowl

She looks like she was sent for but couldn't go

Sad enough to make an angel cry

Feel lower than a gopher hole

That's sad enough to bring a tear to a glass eye

He looked sadder than a hog in a washtub

SAFE

Safe as tucked between the pages of a Bible

No place safer than behind mama's apron

Safe as bein' in St. Peter's back pocket

Safe as a church

Safe as a baby in its mama's arms

Safe as a banker's wallet

SALESMAN

Peddler

He could sell popsicles to an Eskimo

He could sell an air conditioner to an Eskimo

He could sell Satan to a preacher

He could sell sheep to a cattleman

Drummer

He could sell kindlin' wood to the devil himself

He could sell Bibles to the devil

He could sell pork roast to a hog

He could sell snowshoes to a rattlesnake

He could sell sand to a West Texas cotton farmer

SCARCE

Scarce as preachers in paradise

Scarce as snake feathers

Scarce as grass in a hog wallow

Scarce as a snowcone in Hades

Scarce as hen's teeth

Scarce as frog hair

Scarce as gone

Scarce as hair on a rattlesnake

Scarce as hog tracks on a linen tablecloth

Scarce as horse manure in a four-car garage

Scarce as sinners in heaven

SCARED

Scared stiff

Hair-raisin' scared

Would make the hair stand up on a fur coat

Shakin' in his boots

Panicked

Boogered

Scared the beejesus out of him

Put the fear of God in him

Scared clear into Sunday school

Scared him so bad he swallowed his tobacco

Scared his heart into his mouth

Turned his knees to puddin'

He was so scared his blood clabbered

Runnin' away with his tail tucked between his legs

He done ruined his shorts

Spooked

Scared as a hen in a coyote den

SEARCH

Turn the place upside down

Turn over all the cow chips

Looked from floor to ceilin' and back

Beat the bushes

Looked in all eight directions

Pried up the floorboards

SEASONS

Knee-deep in August

Around cucumber time

The creek-risin' part of the year

Just past the peak of watermelon time

Kitchen-settin' weather

Buzzard-comin' time

Blackberry winter

Indian summer

Corn plantin' time

Fodder-pullin' time

Hog-killin' time
(a reference to the cooler days of early autumn)

Layin'-by time

First frost

Molasses makin' time

Camp-meetin' season

SEX

His comb was a-gettin' red

His horns were so big he couldn't get his hat on

SHARP

Sharp as a razor

Sharp as a tack

Keen as a brier

Sharp as a newborn puppy's tooth

Sharp as a cactus spine

Sharp as a rattlesnake fang

SHOOTING

He could shoot the grease out of a biscuit
without breakin' the crust

He could shoot a gnat from a
pine needle a cornfield away

Burn some powder

Throw a bullet

SHORT

He was picked afore he was ripe

Knee high to a grasshopper

Knee high to a cucumber

Knee high to a rabbit's eyebrow

Knee high to a Coca-Cola can

Knee high to a kneelin' bench

Knee high to a tortoise

Knee high to a gourd plant

SHY

Shy as a mail-order bride

So shy she hides in the shadow of her mama's apron

Shy as a kitten

If she was melted down she couldn't be
poured into a conversation

So shy he wouldn't bite a biscuit

SICK

Sick enough to need two beds

Down in the joints

Sick as a dog passing peach pits

All stoved up

More pains than an old widow

Looks like death warmed over

SINGING

Can't carry a tune in a lard bucket

He ought to carry a poke to tote a tune

Crooning

Wailin'

That tune sounds like you been carryin' it in a shovel

He can't sing 'cause he ruined his voice
a-hollerin' for gravy when he was a young'un

Sings like a banshee

Scarin' the livestock

SLAP

I'm gonna slap you naked

I'm gonna slap you into the middle of next week

I'm gonna slap the daylights out of you

I'm gonna slap you silly

SLICK

Slick as a greased pig

Slick as a peeled onion

Slick as a watermelon seed

Slicker'n snot

Slick as a lizard

Slicker'n a peeled cucumber

Slick as a preacher's tongue

Slicker'n an eel soaked in forty-weight oil

Slick as a hound's bottom

Slick as owl manure on a glass doorknob

Slicker'n a pot of boiled okra

SLOW

Slow as an old cow

Slow as smoke off a manure pile

Slow as suckin' molasses through a straw

Slower than sorghum at Christmastime

Slower than molasses in winter

Slower than pond water

He was so slow you would of thought
he was draggin' an anchor

So slow he could gain weight walking

She walks so slow you had to set stakes
just to see if she was a-movin'

He was so slow you could of timed him
with a calendar

Slow as grass growin'

He's one day ahead of yesterday

Too slow to catch a cold

Slow as suckin' clabber through a straw

Slow as Christmas

SMALL

Fryin' size

Knee high to a grasshopper

No bigger than a pissant

Big as a minute

Bite size

Fryin' pan size

Half as big as a minute

He's so small he'd have to stand on a
ladder to look a snake in the eye

Pocket size

Whittled down to a point

He don't amount to a poot in a whirlwind

Tee-ninesy

Small as the end of nothin'

Pint sized

Not enough room to cuss a cat without
gettin' hair up your nose

Only as big as a drop in a bucket

No bigger than a mouthful for a tick

He could take a bath in a green gourd

SMART

Smart as a hoot owl

Bright as a penny

That boy's got rawhide wisdom

His mama didn't raise no fool

No flies on him

Smart as a whip

He don't eat no bugs

That's one coon you can't tree

He can show 'em where the bear sat in the buckwheat

He's got somethin' inside his head besides nits

He's got a mind like a steel trap

He's got mountain sense

Sharp enough to stick in the ground

Smart as a weasel

Smart as a tree full of owls

Smart as a bunkhouse rat

He don't use up all his kindlin' gettin his fire started

Smart enough to bell a buzzard

SMELL

Sweet as honeysuckle

Sweet as a rose

Sweet as a moss rose

Smells like bad meat a half-mile off

He smells like a cow pen

He smells like he's been carryin' goats in his pockets

He smells like the underside of an old saddle

Born downwind from an outhouse

He had a dog that could smell out possums like a
horse-jockey could smell out women

SMOOTH

Smooth as a schoolmarm's leg

Smoother than a baby's cheek

Smooth as a baby's butt

Smooth as a peeled hickory branch

Smooth as silk

Smooth as a hound's bottom

Smooth as polished marble

Smoother'n bark on a Texas madrone

SOFT

Soft as a butterfly's nose

Soft as a butterfly's belly

Soft as a pulled cotton boll

Soft as a mouse's belly

Soft as a two-minute egg

Soft as a honeysuckle blossom

Soft as silk

STARE

He could stare a bear down out of a tree

He could stare a hole in a rock wall

Her could stare a hole in a bois d'arc

He's got a stare that would make
a mountain lion nervous

He could start a fire with his stare

SPANKING

Paint his britches red

Tan his hide

Paint his back porch red

Wear out his butt

Play a tune on the seat of his pants

STEEP

That road's so steep you couldn't get over the mountain if you was ridin' a turpentined wildcat

STINK

Stinks like the back end of a polecat

She smells like a dog just come in out of the rain

Stinks worse than a buzzard

Stinks worse'n a dead possum under the porch

Smells like ten cent perfume

He smells like he's been eatin' skunk for breakfast

STINGY

He wouldn't loan you a dollar unless Jesus
co-signed the note

He'd hold on to a dollar bill so tight that
George Washington would turn blue

Tight enough to squeak when he walks

He's got the first dollar he ever made

Skinflint

Tight

Tight-fisted

He'd skin a field mouse for the hide and tallow

He's so cheap he wouldn't pay a nickel
to watch a pissant pull a freight train

She's so tight she crawls under
the gate to save the hinges

STRONG

Strong as a bull

Stronger'n Adam's off ox

Strong as battery acid

Strong as a new rope

Strong enough to move the Rocky Mountains

He's strong enough to throw a T-bone
past a hungry bear

That woman is so strong she'd be hard to tear down

Strong enough to toss an anvil across the Rio Grande

Strong enough to stop a freight train

Breath so strong it would cripple an ox

Breath so strong you could hang wash on it

That coffee is so strong it could walk to the cup

That coffee is so strong it could tan bull hides

Strong as a mule

So strong he can crack walnuts with his toes

Stronger'n an acre of new-cut garlic

STUBBORN

She's got a head like a Collins ram

Stubborn as a mule

Thick-headed

Bull-headed

Anvil-headed

Stubborn as an ox

He'd make a mule back down

Stubborn as a pump handle

STUPID

He's so stupid he couldn't get pigeons to roost

He was behind the door when the
brains were passed out

He's so stupid he uses a shotgun to hunt corn

He was out in the field hoein' corn
when the brains were passed out

He's about twelve cookies shy of a dozen

If brains were ink he couldn't cross a T

He burns green wood for kindlin'

He ain't got sense enough to poke acorns
down a peckerwood hole

He's got the brains of a roach in a bathtub

He ain't got sense enough to bell a buzzard

His brain would fit inside a June pea

Empty-headed

His IQ is the same as his boot size

He ain't got much north of his ears

Rockheaded

Hollow-brained

Leather-brained

He's got sawdust for brains

Bubble-headed

Mouse-brained

Hasn't got as much sense as last year's bird nest

He don't know A from Adam's off ox

He don't know bullshit from bull's foot

SURRENDER

That dog is all done huntin'

He pulled up on the reins

Holler "calf rope"

Raise the white flag

Tossed in the towel

Sold his horse and left town

Cashed in his chips

Gave up the fight

Gave up the ghost

T

TALK

Jaw

Flappin' gums

Chew the fat

Shoot the bull

Long-winded

Chin waggin'

Could talk a coon out of a tree

He could talk a gopher out of its hole

She has a bell clapper for a tongue

She could talk the legs off a chair

Chin music

He could talk the gate off the hinges

He blows his own wind

He could talk the hide off a cow

She could talk the hide off a lizard

He talks a blue streak

He could talk the trot from a horse

She beats her gums to death

He shoots his mouth off so much
he must eat bullets for breakfast

She's got enough tongue for three women

He could talk the ears off a mule

He's got diarrhea of the jawbone

He's a regular flannel mouth

He greased himself with conversation fluid

She could talk a wagon out of a ditch

Leaky-mouthed

Too much tonsil varnish

She's got a case of the windies

She'll talk your ears into stubs

She can talk the hide off a mossback steer

She can talk a gate off its hinges

He could talk a tomato off the vine

TALL

High pockets

He's a long drink of water

There's snow on his hat all year round

Corn tassle high

He has to duck low-flyin' birds

He's tall as the weeds in a widow woman's yard

Tall as full grown corn

TASTY

Larrupin'

My lips are sayin' hallelujah!

Better than fresh cow's milk to a newborn calf

Tickles my tonsils

TASTE (BAD)

Tastes like horses hooves

Tastes like manure

Tastes like a newspaper sandwich

Tastes like wallpaper paste

Tastes like last week's bath water

TAVERN

Saloon

Beer joint

Bloody bucket

Cantina

Roadhouse

Honky tonk

TEMPTATION

Like smellin' whiskey through a jailhouse window

Like a fresh-picked carrot to a horse

Like a dollar bill to a preacher

TENSE

He's got knots in his piggin' string

He's wound tighter than an eight-day clock

He's got nerves pokin' through his skin

Tight as a fiddle string

Tight as a banjo string

Tight as the top strand on a West Texas
barbed wire fence

Tight as a saddle cinch on a bloated horse

THICK

Thick as thieves

Thick as sinners at a revival

Thick as peckerwoods at a deadening

Thick as crows at hog killin'

Thick as worms in a bait gourd

Thick as whores at a buryin'

Thick as bunkhouse chili

Thick as fleas in pot-liquor

Thick as warts on a pickle

Thicker than fiddlers in hell

Thicker than preachers in hell

Thick as mud in the Mississippi

Thick as molasses in January

THIEF

He's got hot hands

He'll take anything that ain't too heavy to carry

You'd keep a fence around your garden
if he lived next door

Sometimes he saddles a horse that ain't his own

He'd steal the door off the hinges

He'd steal the wire off your fence

He'd steal the nickels off a dead man's eyes

He'd rob his granny's grave

THIN

Thin as a rail

Thin as a nail

Thin as thirsty cattle

He could stand under the clothesline during
a rainstorm and not get wet

Thin as a bat's ear

Thin as a moth's wing

Thin as depression soup

His flanks could use some ham and beans

Fish pole high and gun barrel straight

He's so skinny he has to tie an ox yoke to himself to
keep from goin' down the drain when he takes a shower

She's so skinny she could take shade under a clothesline

Thin as chicken skin

Thin as a gnat's whisker

He's so thin he could crawl through the stove pipe
in a white shirt and not get it dirty

Thin as a fiddle string

He's so skinny he could take a bath in a shotgun barrel

He was so thin he had to lean up
against a sapling to cuss

She's kindly lackin' in the hips and shoulders

You'd have to shake the sheets to find her in the mornin'

A walkin' broomstick

Scarce-hipped

He was so thin he wasn't no more than
breath and britches

Her legs ain't no thicker than a spider's

She could take shade under a barb wire fence

She was so skinny it would take two of her
to throw a shadow

T

Thin as a rake

Too thin to send out in a high wind

He was so skinny you could shade his butt with a match

Thinner than a bar of soap after a hard day's washin'

Thin as a slice of boardinghouse pie

THIRSTY

He's so thirsty he'd drink your beer

Thirsty enough to spit cotton

So thirsty you'd have to prime your mouth to spit

Thirsty enough to suckle a razorback sow

Thirsty enough to drink Rio Grande water

Thirsty enough to drink the Pecos dry

THREAT

If you don't act right, the creek'll rise on you

There'll be a new face in hell tomorrow

I'm goin' to cloud up and rain on your head

I'm goin' to stomp a mudhole in your guts

I'm goin' to pull you through a
knothole and back out again

THROW

Toss

Pitch

Chunk

Wing

Heave

THUNDERSTORM

Frog strangler

Creek riser

Gully washer

Pourdown

Stump mover

Trash floater

Dam buster

Clod roller

Cob floater

Duck drencher

Dumplin' mover

TIGHT (STINGY)

Tighter than Dick's hatband

Tighter than the devil's hatband

Tight as a tick

Tight as a tick on a dog's tail

Tight as a new boot

Tight as a drumhead

Tighter than two drumheads

Tighter than sausage skin

Tight as wallpaper on a wall

Tight as the skin on a catfish

So tight he squeaks

Tight as a new shoe

Tight as the stockings on a fat woman

Tight as a wet boot

So tight he squeaks when he walks

Tighter than the bark on a tree

He'd crawl under the gate to keep from
wearin' out the hinges

Short arms and deep pockets

He chews close and spits tight

Chinchy

Close

Close-fisted

Miserly

Skinflint

Penny pincher

Short

Tightwad

Might as well go out and bay at the moon
as ask that skinflint for money

TIME

Noon-mark

A coon's age

Since Gus was a pup

Month of Sundays

Early candlelight

Late candlelight

Lamp-lightin' time

From hell to breakfast

The forepart of the day

The hindpart of the day

A spell

TIRED

Tired as a boomtown whore

Past going

Out of gas and runnin' on empty

I was born tired and had a relapse

My spring has sprung

Chewed up, spat out, and stepped on

One wheel down and draggin' the axle

Looks like ten miles of bad road

Frazzled

My get up and go has done got up and gone

So tired I couldn't holler sooey if the hogs had me down

Tired as a week-old pup

So tired I could sleep on a barbed wire fence

So tired I could sleep standin' up in a snowstorm

Run down, run over, and wrung out

Played out

Tuckered out

Petered out

Drained

Dried out

TOUGH

Tougher than a wood hauler's boot

Tough as a sow's teat

Tough as a sow's snout

Tougher than the law

Tough as the calluses on a bartender's elbows

Tough as a Mexican cowboy boot heel

Tougher than the law allows

He's got grit in his gizzard

Tough as rawhide

Tough as nails

Tough as grit

Tough enough to pick his teeth with barbed wire

Tougher than a night in a Houston jailhouse

He'll pull out your guts and use them for galoshes

He's tough enough to chew a gun barrel

After he whups you, your hide won't hold
shucks in a tan yard

Can whip his weight in wildcats

Tough enough to scoot down a honey locust backward

He's got sand in his craw

He'll make you spit up somethin' you never swallowed

He'll fight for blood, money, marbles, or chalk

He's got an iron backbone and steel ribs

He's got split hooves and fourteen ribs to a side

He'll put a mark on you that won't rub off

She'll put a lump on your head a hat won't cover

He'll throw a punch before the howdies are over

He'll cut your throat for a dime and
give you a nickel back

That town's so tough the sheriff has to hire a bodyguard

He's tough enough to knock you sky-westward
and crooked eastward

TRASHCAN

Slop bucket

Swill bucket

Swill pail

Leavin's pail

TROUBLE

It's like parachutin' into an eruptin' volcano

Like holdin' a skunk by the tail

A hell of a mess

In a pickle

A hell of a fix

It's third and long and his team done
went to the showers

Knee deep in manure with no shovel

Up the creek in a leaky boat

Got his tail in a wringer

Up the creek without a paddle

Up to his hips in alligators

Worse than sittin' on a hornet's nest

The manure's done hit the fan

The fat is in the fire

Standin' in the middle of a stampede

The little woman has done caught me

TRUTH

Gospel

If that ain't true, then God is a possum

That's how the cow ate the cabbage

Straight from the horse's mouth

If that ain't true, then there ain't a cow in Texas

You can take that to the bank

You can borrow money on that

If that ain't true, I'll be a blue-nose gopher

It's a natural-born fact

It's a dead open fact

TRY

Take a chance

Give it a whirl

Try it on for size

Toss it in the creek and see if it floats

Throw this on the wall and see if it sticks

Take hold of it

Take a stab at it

Take a crack at it

Take a jump at it

Take a run at it

Take a shot at it

Run it up the flagpole and see if it works

Go for the gusher

See if you can dance to this tune

U

UGLY

Ugly as a mud fence

Ugly as a mud fence stuck with tadpoles

So ugly the tide wouldn't take her out

Ugly as a gouge

So ugly his mama had to tie a pork chop around his neck to get the dogs to play with him

Ugly as sin

Ugly as homemade sin

Looks like forty miles of bad road

She'd make a freight train take a dirt road

She's ugly enough to stop an eight-day watch

He has a face like the back end of bad luck

Marked for a hog

She had legs like a churn dasher

So ugly his mama took him everywhere so she
didn't have to kiss him goodbye

She looks like she was pulled through
a knothole backwards

She's so ugly she has to sneak up on a glass
of water to take a drink

He couldn't get a date at a chicken ranch
with a truckload of fryers

She was so ugly she had to blindfold the baby
before it could suckle

She's so ugly she could scare herself to death

She could cook naked at deer camp
and nobody would notice

Ugly as homemade soap

Ugly as a buck-toothed buzzard

So ugly she has to sneak up on the kitchen sink

So ugly she has to sneak up on the mirror

She's so ugly the flies avoid her

She's so ugly her daddy would rather stay home
than kiss her goodbye

She was ugly enough to scare a dog off a meat wagon

She looked like she'd been hit in the face
with a wet squirrel

She's got a face built for a hackamore

She has to slap her legs to get them
to go to bed with her

She looks like her makeup caught fire and
someone put it out with an axe

He looks like something the cat drug in
and the dog won't eat

He'd scare night into day

His face would wilt week-old cotton

When she was born the doctor slapped her mother

Her picture is in the dictionary under ugly

He was so ugly his mama had to borrow
a baby to take to church

She was so ugly she had to slip up
on a dipper to get a drink

He's ugly enough to turn sweet milk into clabber

Her face was so ugly her tears ran down her back

UNACCEPTABLE

Don't cotton to it

That don't butter my bread

Nothin' to write home about

I'd just as soon be stabbed

There's another side to that flapjack

There's another verse to that tune

I'd just as soon eat a bug

I'd just as soon hug a rose bush

That dog won't hunt

I'd rather be in hell with my back broke

I'd sooner pick manure with the chickens

I'd sooner eat a wasp nest

I'd just as soon let the moon shine in my mouth

I'd sooner eat a bug

I look forward to that as much as a good case of cholera

Won't sit still for that

That bucket won't hold milk

That bucket won't hold no beer

That boat won't float

That horse won't run

That mule won't plow

UNAVOIDABLE

You got to play the cards you're dealt

That's the way the cookie crumbles

That's the way the cow chip falls

Can't ride around it

You got to dance with who brung you

Come hell or high water

UNHAPPY

She drove her ducks to a poor puddle

She's got a leak in her skimmer

He's seen better days

He carries a cloud over his head on sunny days

UNLUCKY

Everywhere he turns there's barbed wire fences

If he bought a graveyard, people would quit dyin'

If he bought a truckload of pumpkins
they'd call off Halloween

If he bought a truckload of turkeys
they'd call off Thanksgiving

He's wadin' in a muddy stream

Snakebit

He's playin' poker with a cold deck

If it weren't for bad luck he'd have no luck at all

UNPREDICTABLE

Unpredictable as Amarillo weather

Unpredictable as a Mason County jury

Can't tell which way a mule will jump

UNSOPHISTICATED

Just fell off a watermelon truck

Just rode in on a turnip truck

Just rode in on a pulpwood truck

Raised in a sawmill

Raised in a barn

Raised in a hog lot

As mannerly as a basketful of kittens

He thinks a seven-course meal is a
boiled coon and a six-pack

He don't know no more about nothin' than a
dead horse knows about Sunday

UNWELCOME

As welcome as an egg-sucking dog

As welcome as a stampede on a cattle drive

As welcome as a tornado on a cattle drive

As welcome as an Indian attack

As welcome as a bastard at a family reunion

As welcome as a drought

As welcome as an outhouse breeze

As welcome as a porcupine in a nudist colony

As welcome as a wet shoe

As welcome as a skunk at a lawn party

As welcome as a polecat at a camp meetin'

As welcome as a preacher at a poker game

As welcome as a rattlesnake in a prairie dog town

As welcome as a rattlesnake in a sleepin' bag

As welcome as a hailstorm on a young cotton crop

W. C Jameson

U

As welcome as a ham sandwich at a Jewish picnic

As welcome as a cup of coffee at a Mormon reunion

USELESS

Useless as brains in a preacher's head

Useless as brains in a politician

Useless as tits on a boar hog

All vines and no taters

Useless as a one-horned cow

No use cryin' after the jug's busted

He ain't got no more chance than a pig in a dog race

Got no more use for that than a toad has for spit curls

Got no more use for that than a
hog has for a side-saddle

It's like scratchin' a poor man's ass

It's like a hard fight with a short stick

Ain't fit for soap grease

He ain't got no peas on his vine

Couldn't carry a bridle down the street

He couldn't hit a bull in the rump with a bass fiddle

He couldn't make a scab on a preacher's ass

I wouldn't of clicked my gun on him

I wouldn't bust a cap on that

He don't amount to no more than a puddle of warm spit

Useless as a water bucket without a well rope

Useless as reading the Bible to a mule

Useless as a screen door on a submarine

Useless as a windmill without wind

Useless as a bow without an arrow

No account

Gone to the dogs

Useless as an unbaited hook

Ain't worth killin'

He ain't worth the powder
it would take to blow him to hell

He couldn't sell ice water in hell

V

VAIN

She's got more airs than an Episcopalian

Broke his arm patting himself on the back

He thinks the sun comes up just to hear him crow

I wish I could buy him for what he's worth and sell him
for what he thinks he's worth

Vain as a dog with a hemstitched tail

He buys mirrors by the gross

VALUABLE

Worth a patch of oil wells

He's worth a herd of pregnant racehorses

That land is worth as much as if it had diamonds on it

VOICE

She's got a voice like rusty hinges

She's got a voice like a screech owl

He sounds like he gargled with 100 proof alcohol

He talks like he's got gravel in his gullet

Whiskey voiced

Gravel voiced

He's got a voice like an angry bulldog

VOMIT

Toss

Heave

Throw up his socks

Feed the fishes

Urp

Turned wrong side out

VULNERABLE

A sitting duck

An easy target

Vulnerable as a mobile home in a tornado

Vulnerable as a layin' hen in a hurricane

WALK

Mosey

Amble

Footin' it

Movin' on

Sashay

Hoofin' it

Makin' tracks

Pound the pavement

Hit the road

Leggin' it

Beatin' feet

Wearin' out his boot soles

Ride Shank's pony

Ride Shank's mare

WARNINGS

Don't dig up more snakes than you can kill

Don't tip over the outhouse

Whistle when you walk past a graveyard

Whistle when you walk into a stranger's camp

Don't plow too close to the cotton

A dead wasp can still sting

A dead snake can still bite

WASTING MONEY

Throwin' good money after bad

He needs to put handles on his money

He'd buy sapphires for a hog

Like putting a $40 saddle on a $10 horse

Might as well flush it down the toilet

WASTING TIME

Hollerin' down the well

Spittin' in the wind

Preachin' to the choir

Burning daylight

Arguing with a wooden Indian

Arguing with a lawyer

Catchin' some sunshine

Arguing with a preacher

Whistlin' at the moon

Fishin' with an empty hook

Followin' an empty wagon

Barkin' up the wrong tree

Talkin' Greek to a plowin' mule

WEAK

Weak as a kitten

Weak as well water

Weak as a two-day-old pup

WEALTHY

Livin' in high cotton

He's got more than he can say grace over

Runnin' with the big dogs

He's got more money than God Almighty

He's rich enough to eat his own layin' hens

He's got so much money some of it has gone to bed

He don't ride two on a mule

Rich enough to eat fried chicken every day

He has enough money to burn a wet mule

Eatin' on the high side of the hog

He could pay to air condition Hades

WHISKEY

Patent medicine

Snake oil

Tarantula juice

Bug juice

Cowhand cocktail

Coffin varnish

Stomach warmer

Belly fire

Snake bite medicine

Redeye

Memory remover

WIFE

Bed warmer

Dish washer

Better half

Partner

Runnin' mate

The little woman

The old lady

Ball and chain

Check casher

WILD

Untamed

Uncurried

Uncombed

Fuzzy tailed

Ring-tailed tooter

Feisty

WIN

Strike pay dirt

Score

Haul in the chips

Rake in the coins

Shear the flock

Count the cattle

Another notch in his gun

Another scalp on his belt

Another knot in his rope

Another cow in his herd

Another hide on the barn door

WOMAN

Gal

Belle

Skirt

Babe

Chick

Sage hen

Slick leg

Little lady

Pullet

Darlin'

Sweet thing

Angel

Fireball

Jail bait (minor)

Home wrecker

Senorita

More curves than a barrel of snakes

Kitten

WORK

Doin' business

Raisin' blisters

Gettin' dirt under my fingernails

Gatherin' crops

Hoein' the row

Burnin' the fuel

Makin' hay while the sun shines

Goin' like ninety from can't see to can't see

Wearin' knuckles to the bone

Hard at it

Sweatin'

He's a regular wheel horse

He's a stem-winder and a go-getter

WORTHLESS

He's as worthless as a milk bucket under a bull

Worthless as owl shit

He ain't fit to carry guts to a buzzard

Worthless as two buggies in a one-horse town

He ain't worth dried spit

He don't amount to a hill of beans

He amounts to about as much as a notch on a stick

He's small potatoes and few of 'em on the hill

He ain't worth the powder it would
take to blow him to hell

He ain't worth his salt

X, Y, & Z

YANKEE

Blue coat

Fish eater

Blue belly

YELL

Scream

Screech

Holler

Beller

Howl

Bray

Caterwaul

Hoot

Call

Yelp

YES

Absolutely

For sure

For certain

Darn tootin'

You can say that again

Does a bear have hair?

Does a bear sleep in the woods?

Undoubtedly

Is the Pope Catholic?

Seguro que hell yes

Damn straight

YOUNG

Knee-high to a grasshopper

Whippersnapper

OTHER TEXAS HUMOR FROM

That Cat Won't Flush

Wallace O. Chariton

That Cat Won't Flush is an entertaining country dictionary that contains thousands of the "sayings" so popular in the South, West, and anywhere people talk country. Included are short stories and interesting quotations which bring the humorous definitions to life. Unlike other country language collections, this book is arranged in convenient dictionary format according to the normal English meaning so a special country saying can be found quickly for any occasion or purpose. The accompanying cartoons make this collection a dictionary that is every bit as entertaining as it is useful.

288 pages • 5½ x 8½ • softbound
1-55622-175-4 • $12.95

The Funny Side of Texas

Ellis Posey and John Johnson

The Funny Side of Texas is a celebration of that special sense of humor Texans have developed to survive the bad times and help make the good times even better. Every story and illustration is an example of true folk humor, reflecting the unique geographic, historical, and cultural perspective of some of the state's funniest people.

Noted humorist Ellis Posey and artist John Johnson make readers chuckle, snort, and smile as they travel across the state reminding us again that "people are funnier than anybody."

120 pages • 5½ x 8½ • softbound
1-55622-323-4 • $7.95

Texas Politics In My Rearview Mirror

Waggoner Carr with Byron Varner

Former Texas Attorney General and gubernatorial candidate Waggoner Carr has teamed up with Byron Varner to present a fascinating collection of humorous, interesting, entertaining, and true stories about life on the Texas political front. Mr. Carr relives the experiences of a politician who has seen and done just about everything in the politics of the Lone Star State. The book includes more serious information on the role Mr. Carr played while serving as state attorney general during the traumatic days following the Kennedy assassination in Dallas.

168 pages • 5½ x 8½ • softbound
1-55622-314-5 • $12.95

Republic of Texas Press is an imprint of
Wordware Publishing, Inc. • 2320 Los Rios Boulevard • Plano, Texas 75074

REPUBLIC OF TEXAS PRESS

Fixin' to Be Texan

Helen Bryant

Fixin' to Be Texan pokes gentle fun at the Texas mystique and leaves readers in a happy frame of mind. If they are residents of the state, they'll get a big kick out of Bryant's clever way of identifying our most predominant characteristics; if they are new to Texas, Bryant's book will be an essential tool to their understanding the wonderful (and sometimes incomprehensible) behavior of our fine native population.

Helen Bryant is a well-known columnist for the *Dallas Morning News*. Both Helen and her husband, John Anders, also a nationally recognized columnist for the *News*, are the unofficial humorists for the state.

200 pages • 5½ x 8½ • softbound
ISBN 1-55622-648-9 • $16.95

This Dog'll Hunt

Wallace O. Chariton

The ultimate Texas dictionary and a best-seller, *This Dog'll Hunt* contains thousands of popular Texas sayings plus interesting stories and actual quotations. All entries are arranged in dictionary format so the material is as easy to use as it is humorous. This book features an introduction by former Texas Governor Ann Richards. It makes a great gift for displaced Texans who don't want to forget how we really talk in the Lone Star State.

300 pages • 5½ x 8½ • softbound
1-55622-125-8 • $12.95

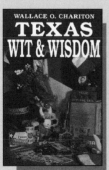

Texas Wit and Wisdom

Wallace O. Chariton

This book is a friendly, entertaining collection of stories, anecdotes, amusing quotations, funny signs, some classic Texas jokes, and even some surprisingly sound advice from the often wacky but always wonderful world of Texans. Features in *Texas Wit and Wisdom* include the bumper sticker hall of fame, amusing T-shirt slogans, and some interesting photographs. This book is a true classic collection of Texas hilarity.

256 pages • 5½ x 8½ • softbound
1-55622-257-2 • $9.95

 Visit our web site at **www.wordware.com**

TEXAS TRIVIA

First in the Lone Star State: A Texas Brag Book

Sherrie S. McLeRoy

"Texas brag" is a long cherished tradition in the Lone Star State. But the fact is Texas does have more than its share of unique people, places, events, inventions, and products—all of them, undeniably, the first, the largest, or the only representative of their kind. *First in the Lone Star State: A Texas Brag Book* is the ultimate "one of a kind" for Texas trivia buffs.

256 pages • 5½ x 8½ • softbound
1-55622-572-5 • $15.95

At Least 1836 Things You Ought To Know About Texas But Probably Don't

Doris L. Miller

Did you know that the city of Borger's earliest jail was a log, and prisoners just sat on the ground chained to it? Or that when Crane County was organized in 1927, the first county officials didn't have a Bible to be sworn in with? They improvised with a Sears and Roebuck Catalog.

Miller has put together a fascinating collection of off-the-wall trivia that could only be found in the Lone Star State. From personal accounts and actual county records, this collection will fascinate even the most knowledgeable Texan.

192 pages • 5½ x 8½ • softbound
1-55622-324-2 • $9.95

A Treasury of Texas Trivia

Bill Cannon

Texas and Texans have been known to boast of having the best or the worst, the most or the least, the largest or the tiniest of just about everything. Join author Bill Cannon as he reveals facts that depict the colorful bravado unique to the Lone Star State. For instance, not six but seven flags flew over Texas. In 1832 the composer of "The Star Spangled Banner," Francis Scott Key, was the counsel hired by Sam Houston to defend him on assault charges. And someone other than Sam Bass may be buried in his grave. *A Treasury of Texas Trivia* is complemented by newspaper accounts, photographs, and other documentation of these and other little-known bits of Texas history.

224 pages • 5½ x 8½ • softbound
1-55622-526-1 • $12.95

Republic of Texas Press is an imprint of
Wordware Publishing, Inc. • 2320 Los Rios Boulevard • Plano, Texas 75074